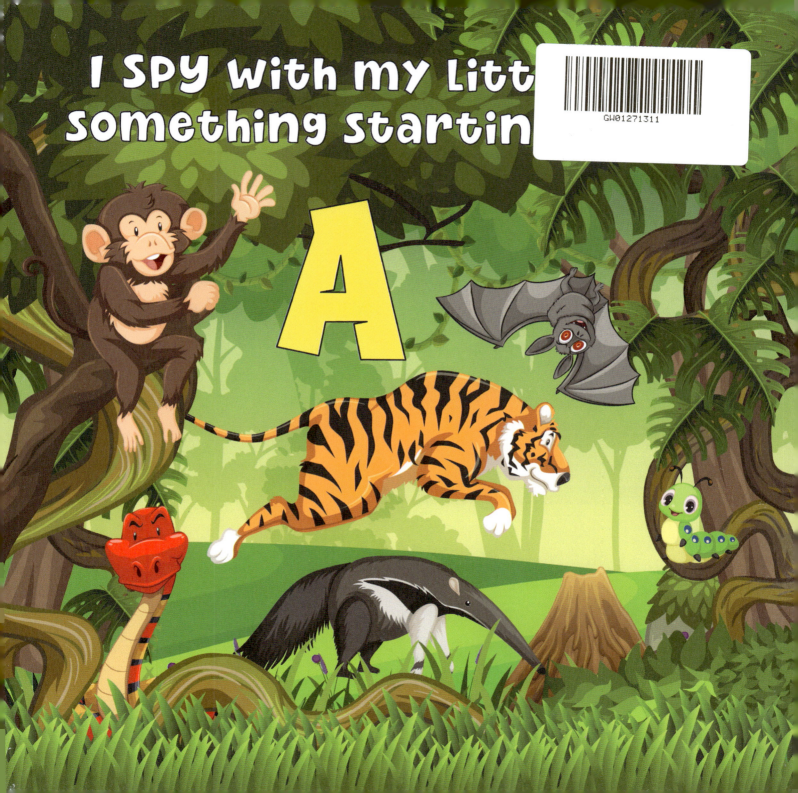

I SPY with my Littl... something startin...

A

A is for

ANTEATER!

B is for  **BEAR!**

I SPY with my little eye, something starting with...

C and D

C is for

CROCODILE!

D is for

DOLPHIN!

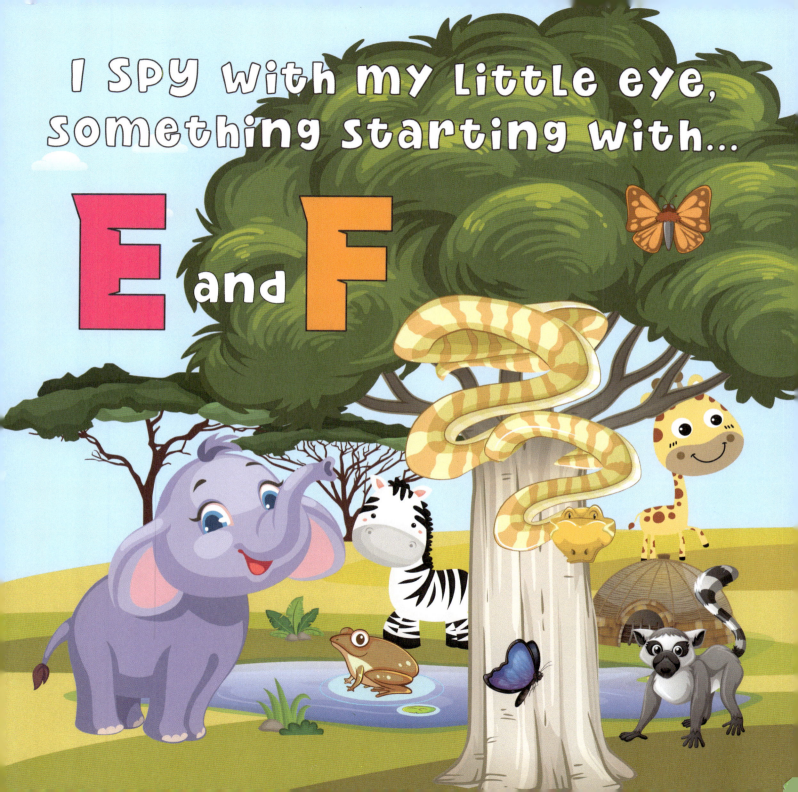

E is for

ELEPHANT!

F is for

FROG!

I SPY with my little eye, something starting with...

G

G is for GIRAFFE! and GAZELLE!

I SPY with my little eye, something starting with...

H

HIPPOPOTAMUS!

H is for

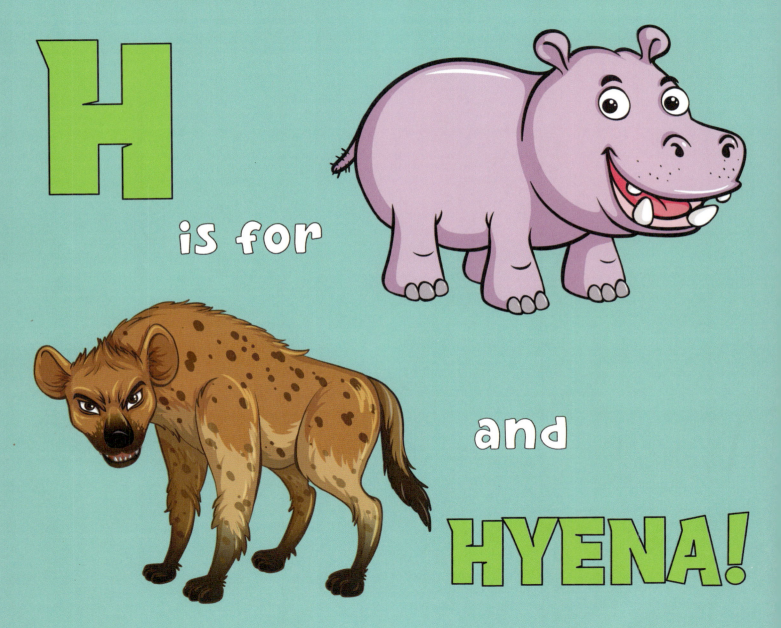

and

HYENA!

I is for
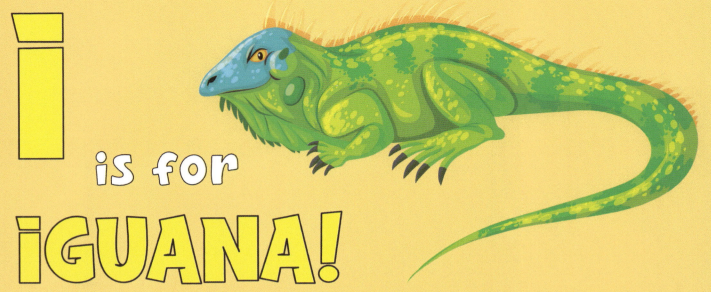
¡GUANA!

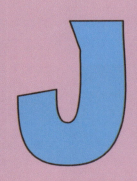
J is for

JAGUAR!

K

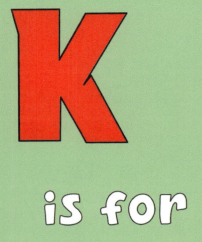

is for

KOALA!

L

is for

LION!

I spy with my little eye, something starting with...

M and N

M is for MONKEY!

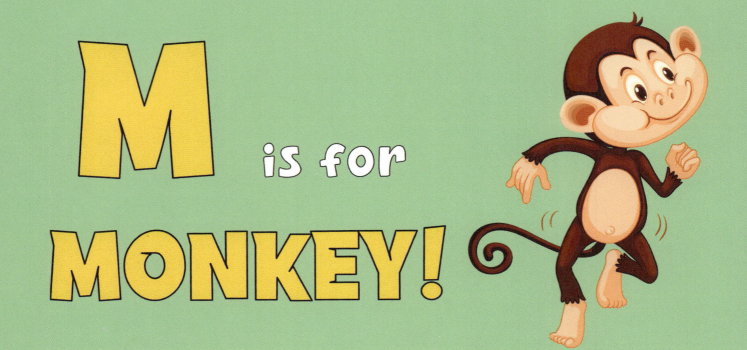

N is for NUMBAT!

O

is for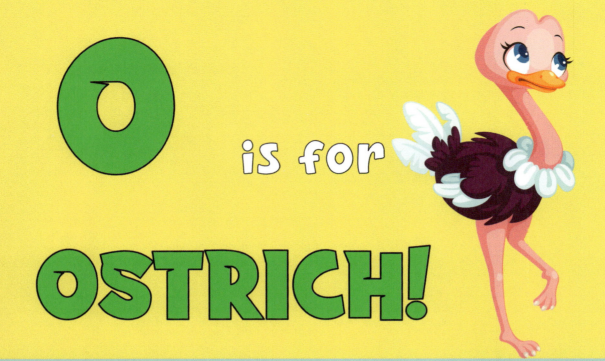

OSTRICH!

P

is for

PARROT!

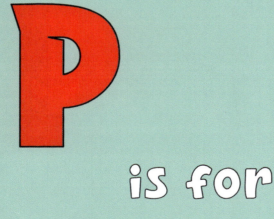

I SPY with my little eye, something starting with...

Q and R

Q is for

QUAIL!

R

is for

RHINO!

S

is for

SNAKE!

and

SLOTH!

I SPY with my little eye, something starting with...

T and U

T is for
TiGER!

U is for
UAKARI!

I spy with my little eye, something starting with...

V is for

VULTURE!

W

is for

WARTHOG!

I SPY with my little eye, something starting with...

X and Y

X 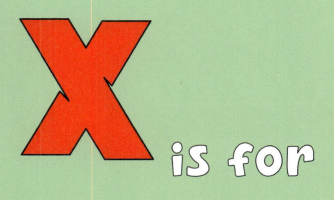 is for

X-RAY FISH!

Y is for

YAK!

I Spy with my little eye, something starting with...

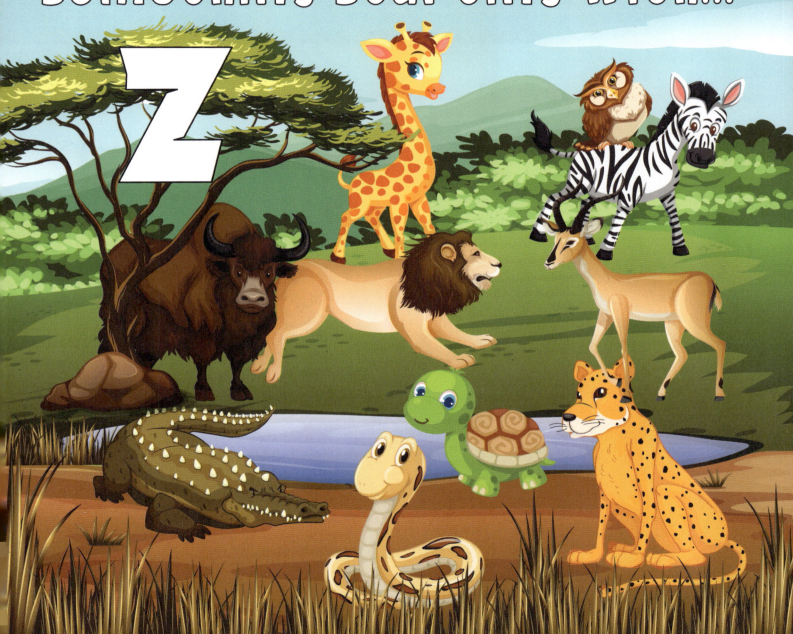

Z is for ZEBRA!

Thank you for getting my book!

If you find this book fun and useful,
I would be very grateful if you posted a review on Amazon!

If you would like to leave a review,
just head on over to this book's Amazon page and click
"Write a customer review".

Thank you for your support!

Printed in Great Britain
by Amazon